TOWER of TREASURE

THREE THIEVES · BOOK ONE

For Miles and Mason
Here, at long last, is the "story with a castle in it" that you asked for.

Text and illustrations © 2010 Scott Chantler

Kids Can Press acknowledges the financial support of the Government of Ontario, through the Ontario Media Development Corporation's Ontario Book Initiative; the Ontario Arts Council; the Canada Council for the Arts; and the Government of Canada, through the BPIDP, for our publishing activity.

Published in Canada by
Kids Can Press Ltd.
25 Dockside Drive
Toronto, ON M5A 0B5

Published in the U.S. by
Kids Can Press Ltd.
2250 Military Road
Tonawanda, NY 14150

www.kidscanpress.com

Pages lettered with Blambot comic fonts.

Edited by Karen Li
Designed by Kathleen Gray and Scott Chantler

The hardcover edition of this book is smyth sewn casebound.
The paperback edition of this book is limp sewn with a drawn-on cover.
Manufactured in Tsuen Wan, NT, in 6/2011 by WKT Company

CM 10 0 9 8 7 6 5 4 3 2
CM PA 10 0 9 8 7 6 5 4 3 2

Library and Archives Canada Cataloguing in Publication

Chantler, Scott
        Tower of treasure / Scott Chantler.

ISBN 978-1-55453-414-2 (bound). ISBN 978-1-55453-415-9 (pbk.)

I. Title. II. Series: Chantler, Scott. Three thieves.

PS8605.H3566T69 2010   j741.5'971   C2009-901521-8

Kids Can Press is a /ⓞⅣS™ Entertainment company

TOWER of TREASURE

THREE THIEVES · BOOK ONE

Scott Chantler

Kids Can Press

ACT ONE
TIGHTROPE

GOD'S TEETH! LOOK AT ALL THE PEOPLE.

IT'S EVEN MORE CROWDED THAN FLAGFORD AND LOGGERHEAD.

FORGET THE *PEOPLE*...THINK OF ALL THE *MONEY!*

I DUNNO, TOPPER...THEY ACTUALLY LOOK PRETTY *POOR.*

NOT DOWN HERE, YOU PUTTOCK.

UP *THERE.*

ALL THE QUEEN'S WEALTH. RIGHT THERE IN THAT TOWER.

THEY SAY HER TREASURY HOLDS MORE GOLD THAN A DRAGON'S DEN.

BUT IF I *DID*, IT'D BE A GREAT WAY TO SOLIDIFY MY REPUTATION AS—

—AS "THE GREATEST THIEF IN NORTH HUNTINGTON"?

PFFT. THE ONLY PERSON I'VE EVER HEARD SAY THAT IS *YOU.*

PEOPLE SAY IT ALL THE TIME!

WHAT PEOPLE?

LOTS OF PEOPLE.

AND JUST HOW WOULD *YOU* KNOW WHERE THE QUEEN'S TREASURY IS, ANYWAY?

MAYBE— JUST MAYBE— I HAVE A *MAP OF THE PALACE.*

I'M SURE I'LL FEEL SORRY FOR ASKING, BUT WHERE'D YOU GET IT?

I BOUGHT IT YEARS AGO FROM A COOK WHO WORKED IN THE PALACE KITCHEN.

OKAY. SO HOW WOULD THE *COOK* KNOW WHERE THE TREASURY IS?

HE WOULDN'T. BUT HIS BROTHER KNEW A GUY WHO CARRIED SOME GOLD UP THERE ONCE.

"HIS *BROTHER* KNEW A *GUY*"...?

I WAS RIGHT...I'M SORRY I ASKED.

13

14

NOT MUCH OF AN AUDIENCE FOR SUCH A LARGE CITY...

DO YOU SEE HIM, DEAR?

WHICH ONE?

WELL...EITHER OF THEM, I GUESS.

ONLY WHEN I *CLOSE* MY EYES.

WHERE IS THE BOY?

WHERE ARE YOU HIDING HIM, WOMAN? I WON'T ASK AGAIN.

I WON'T GIVE UP MY SON.

NOT TO YOU.

THEN MAYBE HE'LL GIVE *HIMSELF* UP.

SIR?

BURN THE HOUSE.

THAT'S AN *ORDER*, MEN.

BURN IT.

AND NOW, GOOD PEOPLE OF KINGSBRIDGE, FOR OUR FINAL PERFORMER...

DESSA.

...A YOUNG ACROBAT WHOSE DEXTERITY HAS THRILLED AUDIENCES FROM HANBROOK TO MAGISHEAD...

...AND WHO WILL SKILLFULLY ATTEMPT TO WALK THE ROPE THAT YOU NOW SEE SUSPENDED HIGH ABOVE THIS VERY MARKETPLACE!

LADIES AND GENTLEMEN...

DESSA!

...THE ONE AND ONLY DESSA REDD!

CLAP CLAP CLAP CLAP CLAP CLAP CLAP CLAP CLAP CLAP C

DESSA.

FISK.

CLAP CLAP CL

CLAP CLAP CL

YOU KNOW WHAT TO DO, TOPPER.

YOU GOT IT, TUBBY.

SIGH.

WAIT...

HEY!

WAIT!

HEY! WHAT ARE YOU—?

THIEF!

HEY!

WHAT THE—?!

THIEF!

GET 'IM!

THIEF!

IF-IF YOU LIKE WHAT YOU SAW, FOLKS, PLEASE GIVE GENEROUSLY—!

WHERE'S MY BROTHER, YOU MONSTER?!

WHAT DID YOU DO WITH HI—?

OH.

I'M SORRY. I-I THOUGHT YOU WERE SOMEONE EL—.

27

VETERAN
THE WARS
HE SOUTH
T FOR FO

FISK?

OH...HI, DESSA!

IS THIS REALLY WHAT IT'S COME TO, FISK? *BEGGING?*

BECAUSE I DON'T THINK YOU'RE GOING TO DO VERY WELL. THIS ENTIRE CITY SEEMS TO BE BROKE.

HUH?

OH, NO...I'M JUST WAITING FOR TOPPER.

OKAY.

SO WHERE IS HE?

UP THERE.

OH, RIGHT.

THE BIG *TREASURY HEIST.*

LISTEN, BIG GUY, I DON'T REALLY KNOW HOW TO TELL YOU THIS...

...BUT I THINK TOPPER'S PUTTING ONE OVER ON YOU. HE'S PROBABLY BACK AT THE WAGON RIGHT NOW, LAUGHING THE POINTS OFF HIS EARS.

THINK ABOUT IT. I MEAN, HOW WOULD HE EVEN GET UP THERE?

HE CRAWLED IN THROUGH THE DRAIN.

THE *DRAIN?!*

HA!

NOW I'VE HEARD EVERYTHING!

WHY WOULD A *TREASURY* HAVE A *DRAINAGE SYSTEM?*

WELL, OKAY...

BUT THIS IS TOO SMALL FOR ANYONE BUT —

LAST CHANCE, DESSA.

YOU WANNA HELP US OR NOT?

ACT TWO
TRAPS

PLEASE, GUARDSMAN!

JUST A CRUST OF BREAD?

I'M SO HUNGRY!

BAH! SCAVENGING DOG!

AWAY FROM THE PALACE BEFORE WE CLAP YOU IN IRONS!

WHAT'S THE PROBLEM HERE, MEN?

CAPTAIN DRAKE!

N-NOTHING, SIR.

JUST A BEGGAR, SIR.

YOU KNOW HOW THE QUEEN HATES THEM MILLING ABOUT.

YES. I KNOW.

SO UNLIKE HER FATHER.

KING RODERICK WOULD SEND SERVERS TO THE GATES WITH SURPLUS FOOD, AND ORDERS TO HAND IT OUT TO WHATEVER NEEDY SOULS MIGHT BE ABOUT.

OF COURSE, PEOPLE WEREN'T SO DESPERATE THEN.

I-I BARELY REMEMBER RODERICK, SIR.

ME NEITHER. I WAS ONLY A BOY WHEN HE WAS ON THE THRONE.

DON'T LET ME KEEP YOU, MEN.

BACK TO YOUR PATROL.

YES, SIR.

THANK YOU, SIR.

I CAN'T BELIEVE WE'RE DOING THIS! WHAT IF WE GET CAUGHT?

I'M NOT PLANNING ON GETTING CAUGHT.

OH, GOOD. YOU MEAN UNLIKE THE OTHER ONES WHO *DO?*

LISTEN, IF YOU'D RATHER CLIMB BACK DOWN AND WANDER THE STREETS LOOKING FOR FOOD, I'M SURE FISK WOULD BE HAPPY TO LOWER THE ROPE.

NOW STOP COMPLAINING AND WATCH OUT FOR BOOBY TRAPS.

"BOOBY TRAPS"? THE QUEEN'S TREASURY IS *BOOBY-TRAPPED?*

WOULDN'T *YOURS* BE?

GOOD POINT.

SO, WHAT ARE THE TRAPS? AND WHERE ARE THEY?

YOUR MAP DOESN'T **SAY?**

UGH.

THE COOK'S BROTHER'S FRIEND NEVER ACTUALLY SET FOOT IN THIS TOWER, DID HE?

SURE HE DID!

THE TRAPS WERE *JUST DISARMED* THEN, SO THEY COULD BRING THE GOLD UP! HOW WOULD *HE* KNOW WHAT THEY ARE?

MAKES SENSE...I GUESS.

SO, WHAT ARE WE LOOKING FOR? TRIP WIRES? FALSE FLOORS?

TAP TAP

...NOTHING THAT SOPHISTICATED, I DON'T THINK.

PROBABLY MORE LIKE—

Click!

THUNK

39

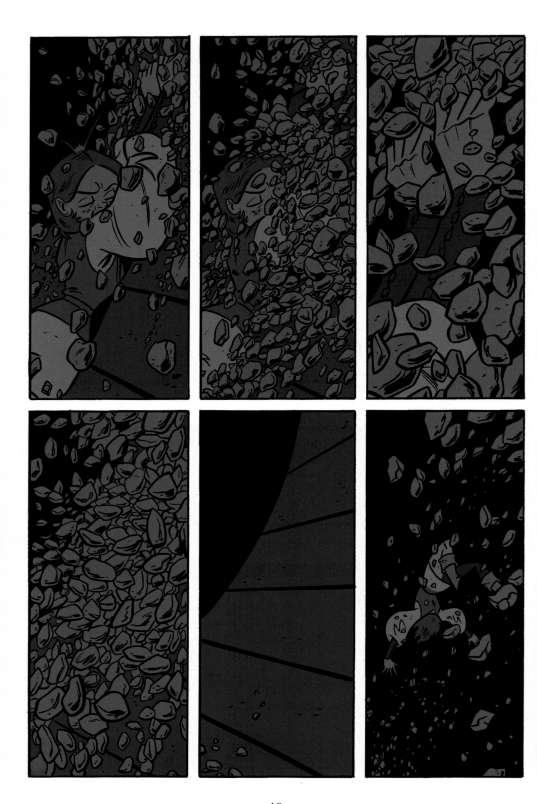

OOOF!

OKAY.

NOW WHAT?

I'VE GOT AN IDEA.

THAT'S WHAT I WAS AFRAID OF.

AND I DON'T LIKE THE LOOK OF THOSE GARGOYLES.

GIMME THAT TORCH.

TAP

WHOOOOOSH

SO, WHAT DO WE DO NOW?

THERE MUST BE A WAY TO DISARM IT.

THERE IS...

46

OPEN THAT DOOR!

SIR?

OPEN IT!

THERE'S SOMEONE IN THE TOWER.

THE QUEEN MIGHT AS WELL HAVE *BLIND MEN* GUARD THIS DOOR.

THERE MUST BE SOME MISTAKE, SIR.

WE HAVEN'T LET ANYONE P—

SUMMON AS MANY OTHER GUARDS AS YOU CAN. I WANT EVERY AVAILABLE MAN. DO IT QUICKLY.

AND YOU...

...GO FIND *MAARTEN GREYFALCON.*

SEE, DESSA?

I *TOLD* YOU WE COULD USE YOUR SKILLS!

YEAH? SO IF *HE'S* THE STRONGMAN AND *I'M* THE ACROBAT, WHAT'RE *YOU?*

I'M THE ONE WITH THE *MAP!*

SNATCH!

OKAY, SO IF WE BELIEVE THE COOK'S BROTHER'S WHATEVER, THE DOOR TO THE TREASURE CHAMBER SHOULD BE RIGHT...

...HERE.

WOOO-HOOO!

WE'RE RICH! RICH, I TELLS YA!

I CAN'T BELIEVE IT...

...QUEEN MAGDA HAS ALL THIS JUST *SITTING* HERE, WHILE HER PEOPLE ARE DOWN THERE GOING HUNGRY.

WELL, NO MORE GOING HUNGRY FOR *US*!

AND NO MORE PERFORMING LIKE MONKEYS FOR THAT FAT CANKER-BLOSSOM AND HIS THIRD-RATE SIDESHOW, EITHER!

WE'RE RICH!

I DUNNO.

THIS WAS TOO EASY.

"EASY?!" YOU'VE FORGOTTEN THE *STAIRS?* THE *FIRE-BREATHING HALLWAY?*

IF *I* WERE SETTING TRAPS HERE, I'D WAIT UNTIL THE MOMENT THE ROBBERS FELT LIKE THEY'D SUCCEEDED, THEN I'D HIT THEM WITH...

ANOTHER LEVER?

YEP.

JUST LIKE THE ONE IN THE HALL.

SO LET'S *PULL* IT!

IT'LL DISARM WHATEVER TRAP IS IN HERE, THEN WE CAN BEAT IT WITH THE GOLD!

NO!

THINK, TOPPER!

WHOEVER PLANNED THESE TRAPS WAS COUNTING ON US HAVING USED THE LEVER OUTSIDE TO DISARM THE TRAP IN THE HALL...

...SO HE PUT THIS ONE HERE, HOPING WE'D PULL *IT,* TOO. IT PROBABLY *SPRINGS* THE TRAP!

OKAY, THEN. SO WE *WON'T* PULL THE LEVER! WHATEVER MAKES YOU HAPPY!

NOW START FILLING A SACK, AND LET'S GET OUTTA HERE...

...THIS PLACE IS STARTING TO MAKE ME *NERVOUS.*

Click!

NOW WHAT?

WHOOOSH

WHOOOOSH

WHOOOOSH

TOPPER?

WHAT DID YOU *DO?*

DON'T LOOK AT *ME!* I THOUGHT YOU HAD THE LAST TRAP ALL FIGURED OUT, *GENIUS!*

SPLASH

SPLOOOOSH

HA!

WE'RE ALIVE!

UH... TOPPER?

NOT ONLY THAT, BUT ALL THE GOLD IS STILL HERE WITH US!

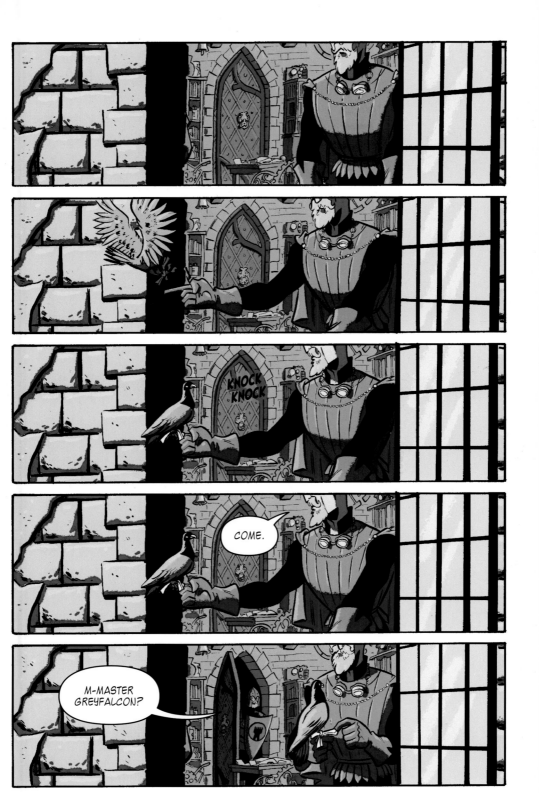

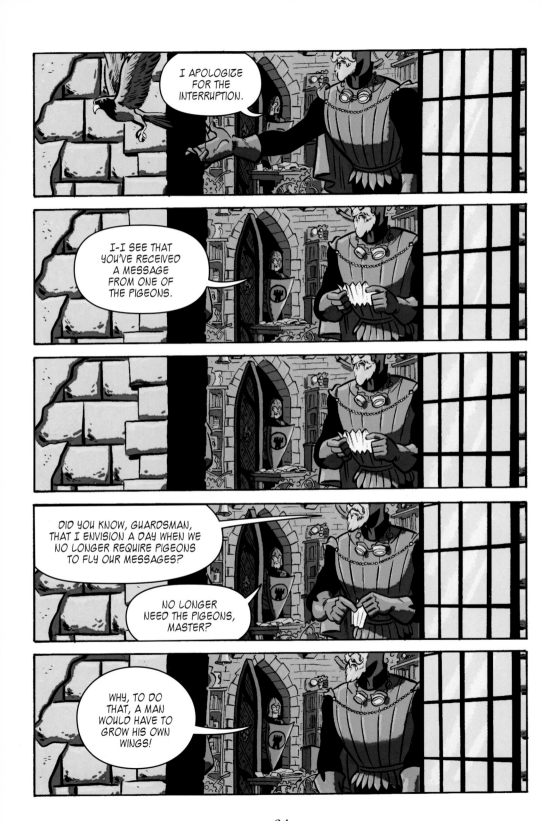

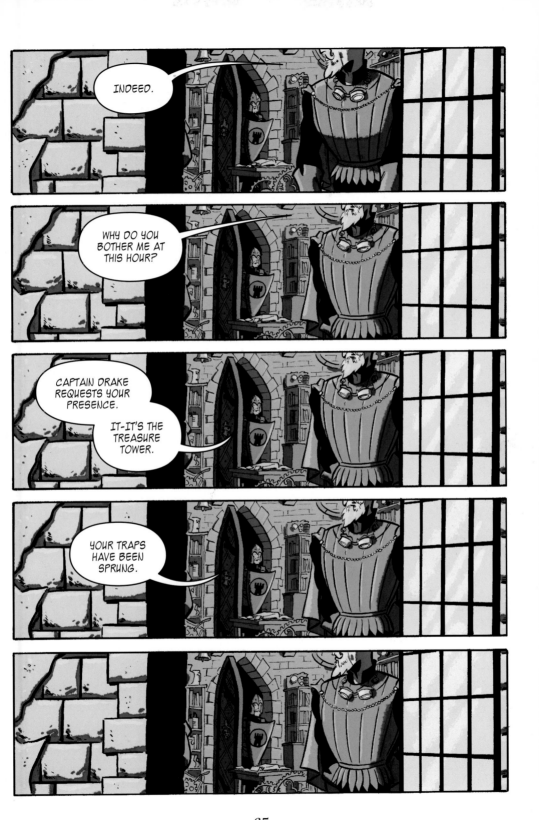

HOW OLD ARE YOU, GIRL?

I DON'T KNOW. I LOST COUNT ALONG THE WAY.

FOURTEEN, MAYBE.

HM. AND WHERE ARE YOUR MOTHER AND FATHER?

I DON'T HAVE A FATHER.

THEN WHERE IS YOUR MOTHER?

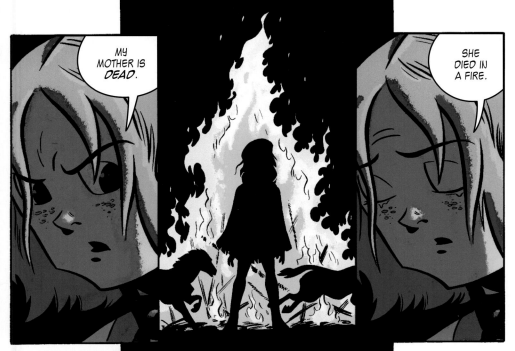

MY MOTHER IS *DEAD*.

SHE DIED IN A FIRE.

I AM SORRY TO HEAR IT.

BUT IT DOES HELP EXPLAIN WHY YOU MIGHT FOOLISHLY THROW YOUR LOT IN WITH A NORKER AND A ONE-HEADED ETTIN.

DO YOU THREE KNOW WHAT THE QUEEN DOES TO THIEVES?

YOU'LL EACH LOSE A HAND TO THE AXMAN.

MAYBE *BOTH* OF THEM.

LISTEN, CAPTAIN ONE-EYE! *NOBODY* GOT ROBBED! WE WERE JUST—

ACK!

BUMP

YOU WERE *SAYING...?*

WHAT HAVE WE HERE, CAPTAIN?

THREE THIEVES, MASTER GREYFALCON. RESOURCEFUL ONES, TOO.

THEY MADE IT ALL THE WAY INTO THE TREASURE CHAMBER, BEFORE GETTING CAUGHT IN YOUR—

YOU.

68

WHERE'S MY BROTHER, YOU DEVIL?

DON'T PRETEND YOU DON'T KNOW WHAT I'M TALKING ABOUT, MURDERER!

WHAT DID YOU DO WITH HIM?!

YOUR... BROTHER?

OH.

THIEVERY OF THIS ORDER AGAINST THE QUEEN WILL NOT BE TOLERATED. WE MUST MAKE AN EXAMPLE OF THESE THREE.

KILL THEM.

WE'LL DISPLAY THEIR HEADS IN THE COURTYARD AS A WARNING TO OTHERS.

THIS ONE IS JUST A *GIRL*, GREYFALCON.

THEN SHE WON'T PUT UP MUCH OF A *FIGHT*, WILL SHE?

LET'S BRING THIS BEFORE THE QUEEN.

I SPEAK FOR THE QUEEN IN THESE MATTERS. YOU KNOW IT AS WELL AS I.

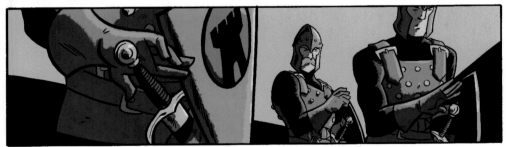

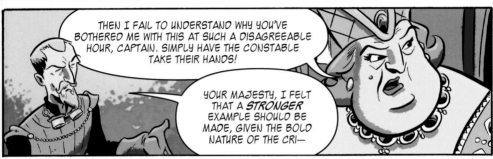

73

AND *KIDNAPPING!* WHAT FOOLISHNESS!

YOU ADDRESS THE THRONE WITHOUT PERMISSION, CHILD, AND OFFER NOTHING IN YOUR OWN DEFENSE OTHER THAN TO ACCUSE MY CHAMBERLAIN OF DEEDS MOST TERRIBLE!

MASTER GREYFALCON'S ORDER *STANDS.*

FOR THE CRIME OF ATTEMPTED ROBBERY AGAINST A ROYAL PERSONAGE, I SENTENCE ALL THREE OF YOU TO BE HANGED BY YOUR THIEVING NECKS, AT DAWN!

ACT THREE

THE CHAMBERLAIN'S SECRET

I'M SORRY I HAVE TO DO THIS.

BUT IF I DON'T, YOUR LARGE FRIEND HERE WILL SIMPLY TEAR DOWN THE DOOR.

AND WE CAN'T HAVE ANY OF *THAT.*

SO YOU'RE *REALLY* GOING TO LET THEM HANG US?

IT'S JUST...THE WAY YOU STOOD UP TO THE CHAMBERLAIN, I THOUGHT—

I SERVE THE THRONE, NOT MAARTEN GREYFALCON.

IF THE QUEEN SAYS YOU HANG, THEN YOU HANG.

JUST LIKE THAT, HUH?

SHE SAYS, "JUMP," YOU ASK "HOW HIGH?"

I THOUGHT YOU WERE A KNIGHT, NOT SOME HALF-PENNY STRUMPET!

MIND YOUR TONGUE WITH ME, NORKER.

IT'S ON MY ACCOUNT THAT YOU STILL DRAW BREATH AT ALL.

I'LL RETURN IN THE MORNING TO SEE THE QUEEN'S SENTENCE CARRIED OUT.

YOU'VE BEEN GIVEN A FEW MORE HOURS TO LIVE. DON'T WASTE THEM WITH FURTHER FOOLISHNESS, OR DESPERATE THOUGHTS OF ESCAPE.

GIVEN YOUR CIRCUMSTANCES, I SUGGEST YOU USE THEM TO BEG FOR MERCY FROM WHICHEVER GODS YOU PRAY TO.

IS HE REALLY GONE?

BECAUSE FOR A WHILE THERE...*WHEW!* I THOUGHT HE WAS GONNA *TALK* US TO DEATH!

YOU'RE GONNA JOKE AROUND NOW?

DIDN'T I *TELL* YOU THIS WOULD HAPPEN? NOW WE'RE GONNA *DIE,* BECAUSE OF YOU AND YOUR *STUPID SCHEMES!*

WE'RE NOT GONNA DIE.

WE'RE GONNA UNLOCK FISK AND HAVE HIM BREAK US OUT OF HERE.

VERY FUNNY. HOW IN THE—?

...SO THEN THE JESTER ASKS THE PEASANT, "ARE YOU A HORSE'S *HOOF?*" AND THE PEASANT SAYS, "NO."

THEN THE JESTER ASKS, "ARE YOU A HORSE'S *HEAD?*" AND THE PEASANT SAYS "NO" AGAIN.

HEH HEH.

"IN THAT CASE," THE JESTER SAYS, "YOU MUST BE A HORSE'S—"

KLUNK!

I TAKE BACK ALL THE BAD THINGS I EVER SAID ABOUT YOU, TOPPER.

YOU REALLY *MIGHT* BE THE BEST THIEF AROUND. THAT LIFT YOU PULLED ON THE CAPTAIN WAS SMOOTH AS SILK.

GLAD YOU'RE HAPPY. NOW LET'S FIND A WAY OUT OF HERE.

YOU'VE STILL GOT YOUR *MAP?*

YEAH, I—

GIMME THAT.

YOU THINK I CAN'T FIND US A WAY OUT?

I'M NOT LOOKING FOR A WAY OUT. I'M LOOKING FOR THE CHAMBERLAIN'S QUARTERS.

WHAT?!

THERE.

DESSA, THAT'S SO CRAZY EVEN I WOULDN'T TRY IT!

YOU HEARD WHAT CAPTAIN UGLY SAID! WE'RE LUCKY TO BE ALIVE!

WE NEED TO DISAPPEAR—NOW—BEFORE THAT LUCK FINALLY RUNS OUT!

HE'S RIGHT, DESSA.

I KNOW HE IS.

BUT DID YOU SEE THE WAY THE QUEEN LOOKED AT GREYFALCON? HE'S INVOLVED IN SOMETHING EVEN *SHE* DIDN'T KNOW ABOUT.

AND IT INVOLVES MY BROTHER, SOMEHOW.

YOU TWO NEED TO ESCAPE, AND I HOPE YOU CAN.

BUT I'M NOT LEAVING UNTIL I FIND OUT WHAT'S GOING ON.

EVEN IF I HAVE TO *DIE* TRYING!

LONG NIGHT, CAPTAIN?

YOU HAVE NO IDEA.

WELL, IT'LL BE OVER SOON ENOUGH.

THE GALLOWS HERE WILL BE READY BY SUNRISE.

YOU FOUND A WAY TO LOCK UP THAT ETTIN?

IT TOOK JUST ABOUT EVERY LENGTH OF CHAIN IN THE CITY, BUT WE MANAGED.

GOT THE KEY RIGHT...

GOD'S
TEETH!

The boy begins to suspect. What are your orders?

WHY ARE YOU SNEAKING AWAY IN THE MIDDLE OF THE—?

SEARCH THE PALACE!

THE PRISONERS HAVE ESCAPED!

GREYFALCON!

THE THIEVES HAVE ESCAPED! THEY—!

KLUNK

WHEW!

HEY!

YOU UP THERE!

GET DOWN FROM THERE, OR WE'LL SHOOT!

UH-OH.

EASY, GIRL...

WHOA WHOA WHOA...

OA WHOA WHOA WHOA WHOA WHOA WHOA

SUN'S NEARLY UP.

I'LL GO TELL CAPTAIN DRAKE WE'RE READY FOR THE PRISONERS N—

WHAT IN THE AVATAR'S BEARD IS *THAT?!*

HEY!

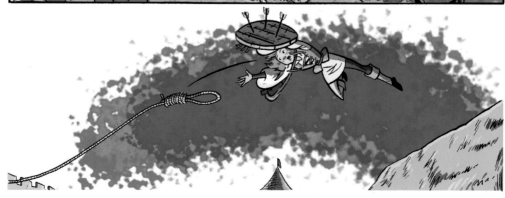

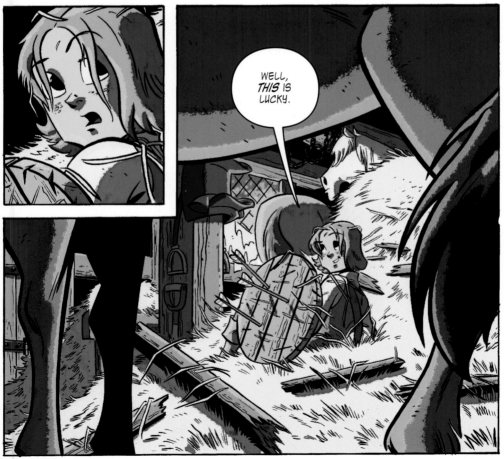

SHE'S HEADED FOR THE WEST GATE.

CHUK

RUMBLE RUMBLE RU—

"FIRST, YOU WAKE ME IN THE MIDDLE OF THE NIGHT TO SETTLE A SENSELESS DISPUTE BETWEEN YOURSELF AND MAARTEN GREYFALCON..."

"...THEN YOU ALLOW THREE PRISONERS TO ESCAPE BY LETTING A TWO-BIT PICKPOCKET GET THE BETTER OF YOU..."

"...AND NOW YOU TELL ME THAT THE ROYAL CHAMBERLAIN IS NOWHERE TO BE FOUND!"

OUTRAGEOUS!

MY FATHER THOUGHT YOU THE GREATEST OF ALL HIS KNIGHTS, CAPTAIN DRAKE. AS DO I. YOUR LOYALTY TO ME, AND TO HIM, HAS BEEN EXEMPLARY.

BUT YOU'VE FOULED THIS UP MOST HORRIBLY.

TO ALLOW US TO BE MADE FOOLS OF, AND BY A MERE *GIRL!*

WITH ALL DUE RESPECT, YOUR MAJESTY, THIS IS NO MERE GIRL. THE MEN SAY SHE MOVES LIKE A CAT. AND SEEMS TO HAVE AS MANY LIVES.

105

SHE'S NOT SOME SUPERNATURAL CREATURE, CAPTAIN. SHE IS FLESH AND BLOOD.

AND I WANT TO KNOW WHAT SHE'S DONE WITH GREYFALCON.

ASSEMBLE MY DRAGONS.

ALL OF THEM, MADAM?

ALL OF THEM.

"YOU'LL RIDE OUT IMMEDIATELY. AT FULL STRENGTH."

"YOU'LL SCOUR THE WHOLE KINGDOM, IF YOU NEED TO. CHASE THEM TO WHERE THE EARTH MEETS THE SKY, IF THAT'S WHAT'S REQUIRED."

"BUT YOU'LL NOT RETURN UNLESS IT'S WITH THE HEADS OF THESE THREE THIEVES."

PST.

TOPPER! FISK!

I'M SO GLAD YOU BOTH GOT AWAY!

IT WASN'T HARD. THE WHOLE CITY WAS LOOKIN' FOR *YOU!*

YEAH. DO YOU THINK YOU COULD HAVE CALLED ANY MORE ATTENTION TO YOURSELF?

I'LL TRY HARDER NEXT TIME.

SO WHAT ARE YOU TWO DOING IDLING ABOUT?

WE DIDN'T REALLY KNOW WHERE ELSE TO GO.

WITHOUT THE CIRCUS, WE'RE A BIT DIRECTIONLESS.

I'M GOING **WEST**.

SAME AS GREYFALCON.

I FOUND THIS IN HIS CHAMBER. IT'S SOME KIND OF NOTEBOOK.

IT'S GOT PLANS FOR ALL SORTS OF STRANGE CONTRAPTIONS...

...LIKE THAT FLYING MACHINE THERE.

MAYBE IT'S GOT **OTHER** SECRETS IN IT, TOO.

DARKER SECRETS.

BUT UNTIL I FIND OUT, I'M GOING TO STAY ON HIS TRAIL.

LIKE A BLOODHOUND.

I HAD A HORSE AND SENT IT SOUTH, TO THROW OFF WHOEVER COMES AFTER US.

SO WHEREVER YOU GO, DON'T GO **THAT** WAY.

WELL, WE WERE THINKIN' OF GOIN' WEST, TOO.

WEREN'T WE, FISK?

HUH?

UH...OH, YEAH. WE WERE JUST SAYIN'.

I MEAN, THEY'RE LOOKIN' FOR ALL THREE OF US. MIGHT AS WELL STICK TOGETHER, DON'T YOU THINK?

YEAH, YOU GUYS WON'T STICK OUT AT ALL ON THE ROAD.

THEN WE'LL STAY OFF THE ROAD.

BUT THREE HEADS ARE BETTER THAN ONE.

ESPECIALLY IF ONE OF THE HEADS IS MINE, WHICH IS AS GOOD AS THREE HEADS.

HERE WE GO.